# THE DO-IT BETTER BOOK

## OTHER BOOKS BY SHARI LEWIS

KIDS-ONLY CLUB SERIES
(Holt, Rinehart and Winston)

**Spooky Stuff**

**Impossible, Unless You Know How**

**Toy Store In A Book**

**How Kids Can Really Make Money**

**Magic Show In A Book**

**Secrets, Signs, Signals and Codes**

**Things Kids Collect**

**Magic for Non-Magicians**
with Abraham B. Hurwitz (J. P. Tarcher)

**The Tell It-Make It Book** (J. P. Tarcher)

**Folding Paper Puppets**
with Lillian Oppenheimer (Stein & Day)

**Folding Paper Toys**
with Lillian Oppenheimer (Stein & Day)

**Folding Paper Masks**
with Lillian Oppenheimer (Dutton)

**Making Easy Puppets** (Dutton)

**Fun with the Kids** (Doubleday)

**Dear Shari** (Stein & Day)

**Be Nimble, Be Quick**
with Jacquelyn Reinach (McGraw-Hill)

**Knowing and Naming**
with Jacquelyn Reinach (McGraw-Hill)

**Thinking and Imagining**
with Jacquelyn Reinach (McGraw-Hill)

**Looking and Listening**
with Jacquelyn Reinach (McGraw-Hill)

# THE DO-IT BETTER BOOK

**by Shari Lewis**

Illustrations by Mel Keefer
Art Direction by John Brogna
Research Coordinator, Sy Kasoff

HRW BOOKS

Holt, Rinehart and Winston
New York

Published by Holt, Rinehart and Winston, 383 Madison Avenue, New York, New York 10017. Published simultaneously in Canada by Holt, Rinehart and Winston of Canada, Limited.

Library of Congress Cataloging in Publication Data

Lewis, Shari.
The do-it-better book.
(Kids-only club)
Includes index.
SUMMARY: The author offers advice, based on information given by experts in their various fields, on how to do particular activities more skillfully. Includes such activities as gymnastics, swimming, drawing, training animals, and taking photographs.
1. Amusements—Juvenile literature. 2. Sports for children—Juvenile literature. [1. Amusements. 2. Sports] I. Title.
GV182.9.L48 790.1'922 79-3839
ISBN 0-03-049721-3
ISBN 0-03-049726-4 (pbk.)

Printed in the United States of America
10 9 8 7 6 5 4 3 2 1

# Dedication

I dedicate this book to Sandy Meisner of the Neighborhood Playhouse in New York City. He taught me not to worry about whether the end result was better—just to concentrate on each moment along the way.

# Acknowledgments

All my other books have been about puppets, paper folding, magic, games, crafts or other activities that kids like to do. But I've found that there are certain *other* things that many kids want to do better than they do them now.

Some of these are activities about which I know very little, and so in each field I've turned to the experts.

Boy, do I have a long thank-you list!

From the bottom of my heart, I am grateful to:

*Cathy Rigby Mason* (Olympic gymnast who now has her own gymnastic schools The Cathy Rigby Gymnastic Academies).

*Ingrid Doland* (swim coach at Westlake Tennis and Swim Club, Los Angeles).

*Michael Fleming* (former U. S. National Figure Roller Skating Champion).

*Dr. Allen Selner* (director, Sports Medicine for the U. S. Amateur Confederation/Roller Skating).

*Roy Smalley* (All-Star shortstop, 1979, Minnesota Twins Baseball Club).

*Gerri Schulman* (head of the physical education department of Virgil Junior High School, Los Angeles).

*Mark Danna* (coauthor of *Frisbee Players' Handbook*, and former National Frisbee Champion).

*Howard Post* (cartoonist/creator of "The Dropouts"—United Features—and many animated TV shows).

*Moe Di Sesso* (a leading trainer of animals for TV and films).

*Scott Brown* (supervisor of training for Dogs for the Deaf in Applegate, Oregon).

*Dick and Enid Grossman* (expert dog trainers in California).

*Joe Fish* (Aquarium Stock Company, Los Angeles).

*Irv Desfor* (*Camera Angles* columnist for Associated Press for thirty-one years).

*Marty Ragaway* (TV comedy writer, publisher of *Funny Funny World*, a newsletter about the funny things happening all over the world).

*Michael Binder* and *David Couwlier* (both excellent young comics from The Comedy Store in Los Angeles).

*Troy Evans* (a professional Hollywood actor and storyteller).

*Sy Kasoff* (research coordinator).

*Mel Keefer* (cartoonist for many feature strips—currently RICK O'SHAY, *Chicago Tribune Syndicate*—and animator of TV series for major cartoon studios).

# Contents

Barker
FOTO FUN
Shawn
Jimmy
KIDS-ONLY CLUB
Malley
Georgia
Twerp

# Introduction

"Buy your bread from a baker." My mother always used to say that to me. Why? Well, if you buy your bread from, say, a policeman, it's not likely to be as delicious as the baker's. He bakes bread every day and knows all the tricks of the trade.

In other words, my Mom was saying, "If you need something, get it from a pro."

That's what I did for you.

I've found that many kids are secretly unhappy with the way they do certain things. But generally, young people don't like to tell anybody. It's only after I've talked with most kids for a while that I begin to discover how annoyed they are with themselves because they can't draw what they see—or catch a ball without flinching—or do a headstand without flopping over.

Many kids just *know* that their animals could do better tricks if they only knew how to teach 'em. They can *see* that the photos they take aren't as good as they could be. But kids don't know where to turn to learn how to do these things better.

Now, this isn't really a "how-to" book. You can't teach someone how to cartoon or crack jokes or do cartwheels in a couple of pages.

This is a book of tips.

In each field the experts have shared tidbits of information with you. These hints will help you get the knack of it—whatever "it" is that you want to do better.

Often these quickies will make all the difference in the world. (You know how everyone says, "Cats are independent and can't be trained"? Well, wait till you see the tricks Moe Di Sesso uses to train his TV star cats. They'll work like magic on yours too.)

Some of these tips will help you break habits that may have been making it hard for you, habits that may be holding you back. (Perhaps you've been breathing wrong as you swim or holding the ball or Frisbee in a way that's hurting your game.)

And if there's something you're good at, these tips are for you, too. After all, you don't have to be bad at something to want to be better.

The Kids-Only Club gang (Mally, Shawn, Georgia, Jimmy, Twerp and their silly dog Barker) and I don't agree with people who say, "There are no easy ways to do things right."

We hope the experts in *The Do-It Better Book* will show you that the *right* ways are often the easiest.

# 1. Head Over Heels About Gymnastics

Watching gymnastic champion Cathy Rigby Mason perform always makes me feel good. She's not only pretty and pretty sensational—*she's even smaller than I am!* (I'm 5 feet tall, and seeing someone tinier do such wonderful feats makes me think that wonderful things are possible for me, too!)

Cathy competed in two Olympics, and in 1972 she placed higher than any other American gymnast in that competition. She now has her own schools called the Cathy Rigby Gymnastic Academies.

She says kids can get started with gymnastics at school or recreational parks by swinging on the bars, climbing ladders, skipping rope, running broad jumps, doing leg-lifts, chin-ups, and so on. This kind of play uses the same muscles you need in gymnastics.

Fooling around with equipment like ropes and ladder bars also helps you because it builds up calluses on your hands!

Jumping rope strengthens your legs and develops quickness and balance — all needed on the balance beam.

Of course, says Cathy, ballet and tumbling classes are even better, but you *can* do a lot on your own!

First, work on becoming flexible. Here are five exercises that Cathy's students do:

1. *The Bridge:* Lie on your back, palms flat by your

ears, feet tucked in. Slowly raise your tummy as if someone were pulling up a string attached to your belly button.

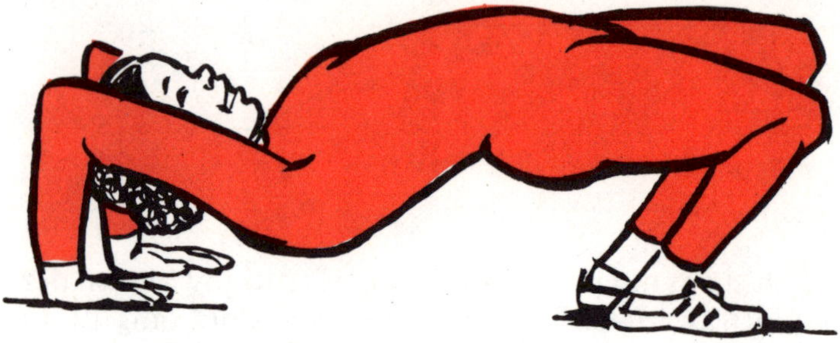

2. *The Jackknife:* Squat down. Stretch your hands out and put them on the floor, palms down. Straighten out your knees so you are in an upside down "V" position. Slowly start walking up. Bring your legs as close to your hands as you can, without straining or hurting yourself.

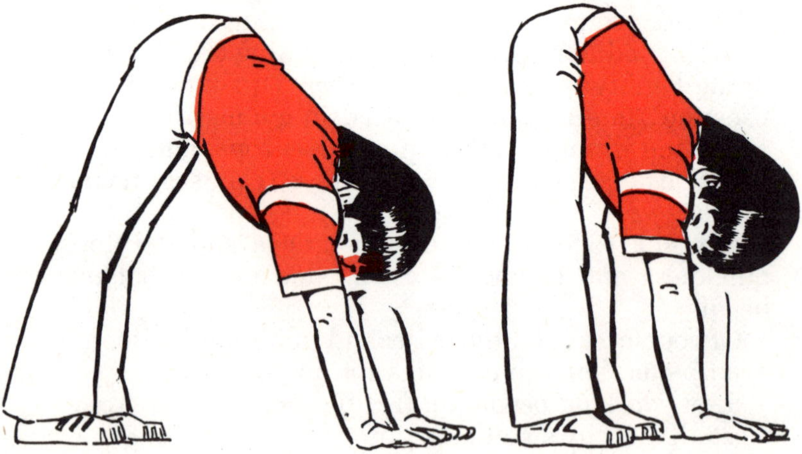

3. *Side Splits:* Draw two chalk lines that cross at right angles to one another. Stretch your legs along one chalk line. Position your hips so they're lined up with the other chalk line. Now lower yourself very slowly. (Don't go too far. After a while, if you do this a little bit each day, you'll be amazed at how far down you can go!) First do this with your right leg in front, then practice it with the left one. Before you know it,your muscles will stretch out and become flexible and this exercise will become easier and easier to do.

4. *Front Splits:* Sit facing a wall. Extend your legs all the way out, feet up and touching the wall. With

your hands, push your body closer and closer to the wall. Just edge in little by little.

5. *The Back Stretch:* To strengthen and stretch your back and arm muscles hold a broom behind you as shown in the picture. Reach both hands back and curve them *over* (not under) the broom. Your palms should be facing back and down (not up). Now lower the broom as far down as you can by straightening your arms and swiveling your wrists slightly. Then bring it up again to the starting position.

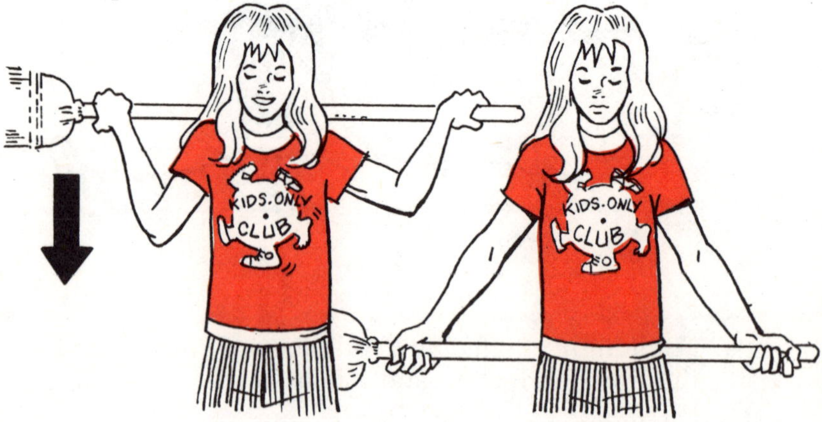

Cathy (and every other gymnast I have ever met) says that the Number 1 Rule is this: ALWAYS DO GYMNASTICS WITH A BUDDY.

Your buddy is there to help you in lots of ways: To protect your head as you try to flip, to hold your waist as you do a cartwheel, to grab your feet as you kick up into a headstand.

What your buddy will *not* do is push or press on your body to help you, say, get farther down into that split. Only *you* know how far your body can go.

**A forward somersault is easy, but how do people roll backward?**

Squat down with your feet together and knees bent, tuck your chin in, put your palms up beside your ears and start rocking back and forth. Don't throw your head back (that's what *I* always want to do, since I know I'm headed backward). Keep the chin tucked in and after a couple of rocks, just roll backward and over you'll go!

**What's the right way to do a cartwheel?**

Draw a straight chalk line. Hold your arms and legs out as shown in the picture.

Stand up absolutely straight with your arms and legs held out like the spokes of a wheel. If anything is out of line, you'll have problems — just as a wheel would.

Since a cartwheel looks like it's all happening in one move, many kids throw their entire body into it. Don't! Actually, you want to hit with each part separately — first your right hand comes down, next your left hand, then your left foot and finally, your right foot. Or if you start with your left hand, next put down the right hand, then the right foot and finally, the left.

Cathy says that in learning cartwheels, your buddy will really come in handy, holding you by the waist as you go over.

**How do you keep from flopping over when you kick your legs up to a headstand?**

For openers, do it near a wall. This will break your fall. Start by squatting. Lean forward and put your hands, palms down, on the ground. Place the top of your forehead (not the top of your head) on the ground, too, so you form a triangle between your hands and your head.

Now, kick your legs up. (It's okay if they rest against the wall, at first.) Once they're all the way up, keep your back straight. Your hips should be in line with your feet and bottom (as they are when you're standing up).

If you have trouble starting, kick up one leg and let your buddy help you with the other.

Now, here's the trick:

—If you feel your legs starting to fall *toward* the wall, press down with your fingertips. That will put you back in balance.

—If you start to fall *away* from the wall—press down with your palms.

**Is it hard to balance up on the balance beam?**
Yes, says Cathy, but you start on the ground.

—Draw a line 4 inches wide on the floor and practice walking on *that*.

—Pretend that the curb is a balance beam. It's about the right width and gives you a little bit of height on one side, at least. As you walk along the street, try to step *only* on the curb.

# 2. Swim Like A Fish!

In Southern California, where the sun shines seven or eight months of the year, there are lots of pools and miles and miles of beaches. Most kids get swimming lessons when they're very young. The rule is "the sooner, the safer."

In fact, I once saw a pair of six-week-old twins being conditioned (can you "teach" a six week old?) to bob up and down in a pool and to breathe whenever their heads rose above the surface of the water! In this way, the babies were safe, even if they accidently fell into a pool.

In other parts of the country where the swimming season is only two months long, many kids don't get real swim lessons. They tell me they've just picked it up themselves, and they muddle through summer after summer, never really feeling free and easy in the water.

Ingrid Doland, swim coach at the Westlake Tennis and Swim Club, specializes in helping kids (sometimes even very little kids) get the hang of it.

Here are some hints she shares with young people every day in answer to their questions.

**When you put your face in the water or swim under water, how do you hold your breath so long?**

You *don't* hold your breath. Ingrid says that the minute your face goes into the water, you BREATHE OUT! If you hold your breath, you trap carbon dioxide in your body. That makes your muscles tired. Besides, exhaling is very relaxing.

Try it. Put your face in the water and blow out air. You will hear a bubbling sound as the bubbles rush past your ear.

Ingrid feels that most people are afraid they won't have enough air. The truth is, you needn't be in a hurry to take the next breath. You can prove this to yourself. Here's how:

> Sit on dry land. Hold your breath. Use a stop-watch and keep track of how long you can do it. You'll discover a couple of things:
> —Holding your breath without breathing out is really tiring.

—You can hold it a lot longer if you *do* exhale. Now get into the water. Mark off the farthest distance you feel you can swim. Count how long it takes you to do it. Ingrid is certain you will discover that *you can hold your breath much longer than you need to* in order to go that distance. So if you miss a breath or two along the way, you'll still be able to make it with ease.

**How can you see where you're going with your head in the water?**

Keep your eyes open! If you do, you'll know *just* where you are, and that will make you feel like you belong there. She says kids under the age of four do it naturally. You may too. Give it a try.

To practice, play "Sunken Treasure":

> Drop pennies into the shallow end of the pool. Then race your buddy to see who can look for and pick up most of the loot.

**What's the Deadman's Float?**

Isn't that an awful name? Luckily the name doesn't seem to scare anybody. Ingrid says most kids float face down without any effort.

Try it in water up to your chest. Your buddy can help you at first by holding his or her hands under your tummy. Now, lie face down and relax. Chances are, you'll float right off your buddy's hands!

**How do you get out of the floating position?**

Don't try to pull your head up. Instead, bring your knees to your chest. That will cause your upper body to rise. From that position, it's a cinch to put your feet down on the bottom.

**What's the right way to kick?**

Keep your legs straight but not like sticks. It's like walking, where as you bring one leg forward, it bends slightly.

When you're kicking, try to use your thigh muscles (above the knee) rather than your calf muscles.

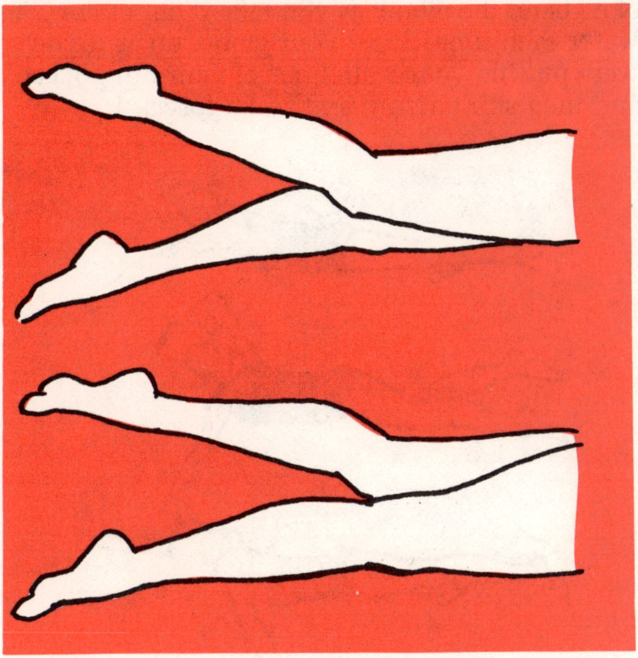

Hold onto the side of the pool and kick.

Next, hold a small float, inner tube or beach ball, and kick away! This is fun because with a couple of good strong kicks you can shoot yourself right across the pool!

**What should you do with your arms? Is there one stroke that you have to learn?**

There are lots of different strokes. Here's a good starter:

> With almost straight arms, imitate a windmill. Make forward circles with one arm after another. Next, try this in the water while floating face down. As each hand goes into the water in front of you, pull the water *toward* your body. Ingrid calls that "the center pull."
>
> Now bend the elbow as you take it out of the water each time. Bring your elbow up as if you were pulling your wallet out of your hip pocket and then straighten it and reach forward.

**You can't keep your head in the water and blow out all the time. When do you breathe in?**

First, find out whether you are more comfortable turning your head to the right or to the left. One or the other will feel right. Stick with that. As you turn your face to one side, one ear will dip into the water (if you roll your face to the left, your right ear will go below the surface).

As you roll your head to one side, your mouth will come out of the water. *That's* when you breathe in, through your mouth. Then turn your head back down into water and blow out, through both your nose *and* mouth.

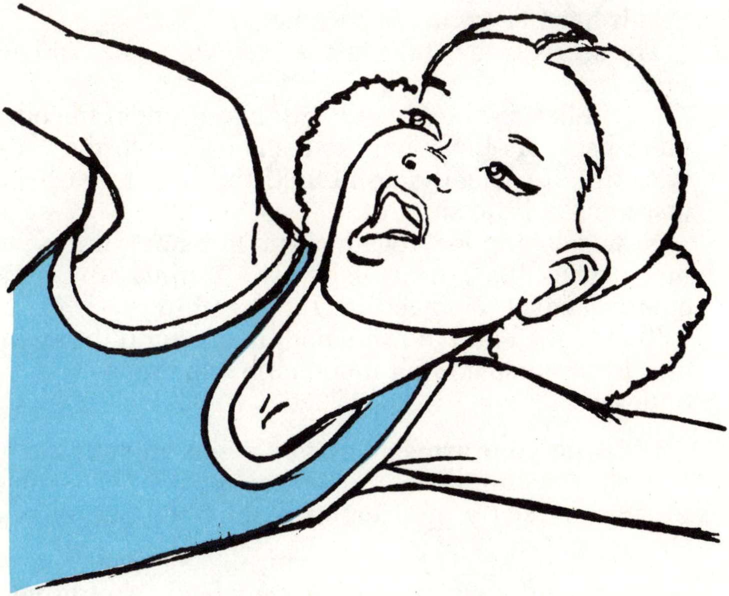

**How often should you turn and breathe?**

Ingrid believes you'll want to breathe every fourth stroke or so, blowing out during the other three strokes.

Find out how often you *feel* like breathing, and stick to that rhythm—otherwise your body may get confused and panic because it won't know when its next breath of air is coming.

**As you roll your head to one side do you peek in front of yourself to see where you're going?**

No. Follow your favorite hand with your eyes as you do that windmill motion. (Your favorite hand is the one on the side you like to turn toward.) Then, as that hand moves forward, your eyes will move forward too. You can see where you're headed as you roll your face back into the water.

**Is it hard to swim on your back?**

The secret is to get the knack of *floating* on your back first.

Ingrid has one buddy put both hands under the other one's back. As the swimmer leans back into the water (face up), the friend doesn't *hold* the swimmer up, but just gives a little support.

Now, keeping feet together and arms out, the swimmer *arches the back, pushes the tummy up — and breathes easy!* (No need to stop breathing.)

Slowly the buddy lowers both hands until the swimmer is happy just lying there, enjoying the view of the blue sky.

**What do your arms do as you swim on your back?**

A slow windmill is a good backstroke, for starters. Breathe regularly, not just any old time. Set an easy pattern and stick to it.

**When you're swimming on your back, should your eyes follow your hands?**

No. In the backstroke, the idea is to *look where you*

*came from*. Pick something at the end of the pool where you started. Keep your eye on that object. Don't look up at the sky as you're stroking because then you'll lose your sense of direction.

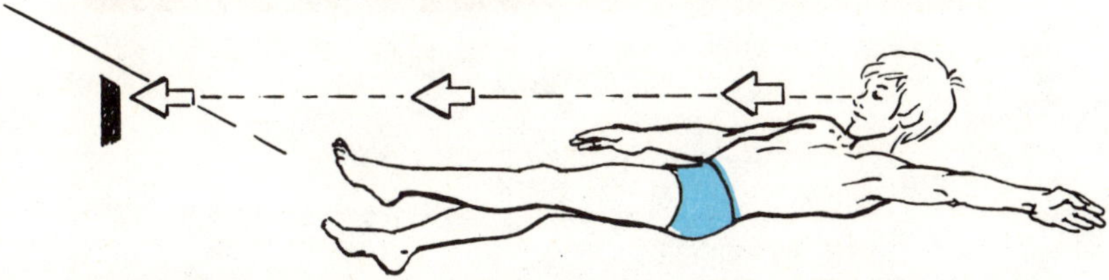

**To get from here to there, can't you just do the dog paddle?**

Better leave it to the dog. Dog paddling is the hardest way to move forward. Since your head is up, your feet will sink lower and slow you down. In that case, what you're really doing is treading water.

**What's the right way to tread water?**

Start by pulling your chin up, looking at the sky and move your legs the way you do when you're pushing bike pedals around and around.

Hold your hands right under the surface of the water, and make believe you're climbing a ladder.

**Is there a way you can jump into the pool without getting water up your nose?**

"Sure," Ingrid says. "As you jump into the pool, snort like a bull." This forces the air *out* of your nose. My favorite leap is the Lifesaving Jump. As I leap into the pool (snorting like a bull), I spread my arms and legs as wide as they can go. When I hit the surface of the water, I smack down very hard—with my arms and outstretched palms—and my head doesn't even go under the water! This is called the Lifesaving Jump because a lifesaver can leap into a lake or a pool and still keep an eye on the person who's in trouble.

# 3. Relating to Roller Skating

**If you want to roller skate well, what kind of skates should you buy?**

Mike Fleming says you first have to decide whether you're going to skate indoors or out. When I talked with Mike (former U.S. National Figure Roller Skating Champion) and Dr. Allen Selner (Director of Sports Medicine for the U.S. Amateur Confederation/Roller Skating), they told me that nowadays roller skates come with polyurethane wheels. You can get your wheels in hard plastic or soft plastic.

—The soft wheels are for outdoor use. They make it easy to roll over twigs on the sidewalk, cracks in the cement, and things like that.

—The hard wheels are for skating indoors (in a rink).

**Should you get high-topped shoes or tennis shoes?**

All the high-topped shoes have good *counters* (that's the part of the shoe that braces and supports your ankle).

Not all the low tennis shoe skates (sometimes called jogger skates) have good counters. They just don't give you the same support.

**Do you have to check your skates every time you put them on?**

Before you roll into the rink or street, shake your feet

to make sure there are no loose parts that need tightening or fixing.

Make sure your skates are laced right. If they're not, you're liable to wobble inside the shoe, which won't help your balance. Loose shoes rub and cause blisters.

And before you actually start skating, do some warm-up exercises. This will help your muscles to stretch, not tear. (See the exercises in Chapter 1, Head Over Heels About Gymnastics.)

**O.K., you're in your skates. What do you do first?**

Mike Fleming says to start with your feet together. Then push off onto one foot. Lift the back foot. Now put both feet together again and push off on the other foot. Bring them together again—and so on. He says you'll soon get the feel of the wheel.

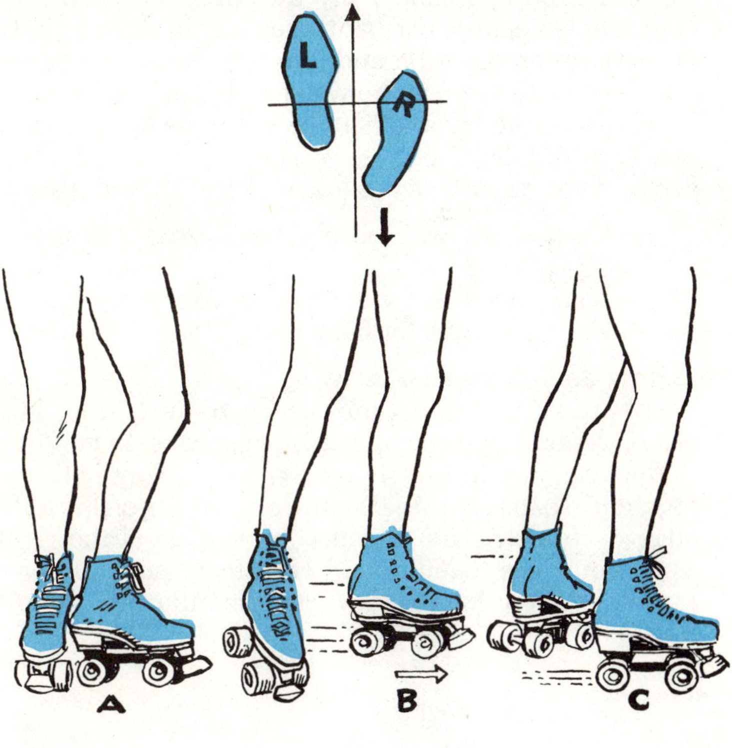

**Is skating like walking, but on wheels?**

No! The experts say skating is different from walking in a number of ways:

—When you walk, you put one foot in front of the other. But when you skate, you leave one foot *behind* the other, as it helps you to push and to balance.

—As you walk, your weight stays right in the center of your body. In skating, all your weight shifts to the foot you're standing on. (Your free foot is up in the air, because you've used it for pushing off.)

**Some skaters hunch over like gorillas. Others stand up and glide along. What's the best skating position?**

Some skating teachers say the safest position for a beginner is a bent-waist, bent-knee way of skating (like a cross between a gorilla and Groucho Marx). They feel that leaning forward at the waist and bending the knees helps you avoid back falls (which are the most dangerous kind of falls).

*All* of the experts agree that a skater should always:

—Keep knees bent loosely (not locked into any one position).
—Look ahead, and not down at your feet.
—Use your arms for balance.

**How do you make a turn?**

Put pressure on either the outside or the inside of the skate, depending on which way you want to go.

An easy way to turn is by *coasting*. Bring both feet together. To turn to the left, put your weight on the outer edge of the left skate and the inner edge of the right. Keep your legs together and your feet, too, and you'll smoothly curve to the left. (Lean the other way to turn right.)

**What should you do if you feel like you're going to fall?**

Stay loose! Let yourself get limp. Roll as you fall. *Don't try to break your fall by sticking out your arms or hands.* You want your body to take the impact, so just become a ragdoll and take it in your stride!

And (says Mike) if you're skating in a rink, *get up quickly*. Others will be barreling along behind you, and you'll want to get out of their way.

**When you try to get up, how do you keep your skates from sliding out from under you?**

When you fall, quickly get into a kneeling position. Put one foot underneath you, with your weight on the toe stop. (Shoe skates have rubber toe stops that grip the floor.) You'll be able to get up from this position.

**When you're sailing along on skates and want to stop, what do you do?**

Put your weight on your strongest leg. Place your

*When you place your weight on one foot, the other comes off the ground.*

other foot behind that leg so that your two skates form the letter "T." Gently lower the back skate to the floor,

*This is the T-stop position.*

keeping your feet close together. Slowly transfer your body weight from the front foot to the back one. The back foot will be sliding sideways. The rubbing caused by that sliding skate will act as a brake.

**Is skating backward as scary as it looks?**

Not according to Dr. Selner and Mr. Fleming. They say you may even like it better.

It's *different* from forward skating. When you skate backward *you generally stay on two feet.*

—Start by holding onto something: a railing, a wall, or a friend.

—Make yourself pigeon-toed (toes in, heels out).

—Bend your knees and slowly push yourself off.

—*Push your feet apart by leaning on the inside of each skate.*

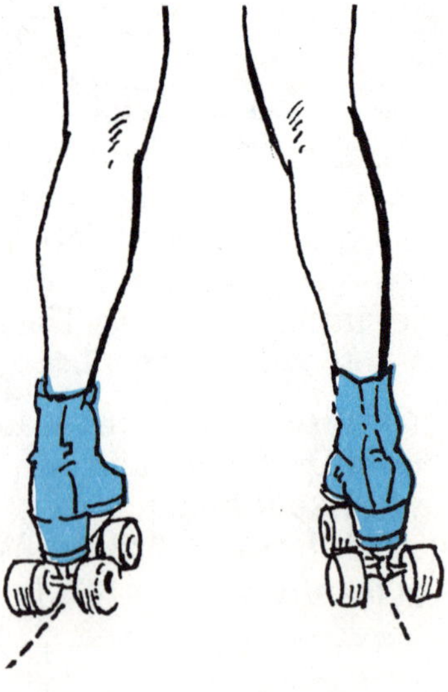

—When your feet are about a foot apart (the space between them should be about as wide as your shoulders), start pulling your heels together.

—When your heels are only a few (3 or 4) inches apart, start pushing the heels apart again, as you did in the beginning.

Using this "scissors" motion, you'll be flowing right along—backward!

**When you're skating backward, do you stop in the same way as when you're skating forward?**

No. Bring both feet together and put pressure on both toes. The toe stop will bring you to a halt.

**What kind of tricks can you try?**

If you have strong stomach muscles, you might try "Shooting the Duck." Here's how:

—Glide forward, with both skates facing in the same direction (parallel).

—Squat down into a deep knee bend as you glide.

—While rolling in this sitting position, hold your arms out in front of you.

—Now (if you can) put one *leg* straight out in front of you, too.

It isn't hard, but it does take strength. If you have trouble keeping your balance, grab the leg that's sticking out with both hands. Don't let the skate on the leg that's sticking out touch the ground!

# 4. Throwing and Catching

## THROWING

Roy Smalley of the Minnesota Twins Baseball Club (and All-Star shortstop in 1979) says that some kids pick up a ball for the first time and just throw well automatically. Others don't. In the same way, some kids just naturally dance or sing better than others. But when kids find that throwing doesn't come easy, they try too hard. They tense up and use too much of the body in order to throw.

**How should you hold the ball?**

The ball should never be held in the palm of the hand. Hold it as close to your fingertips as you can. There should be a space between your palm and the ball.

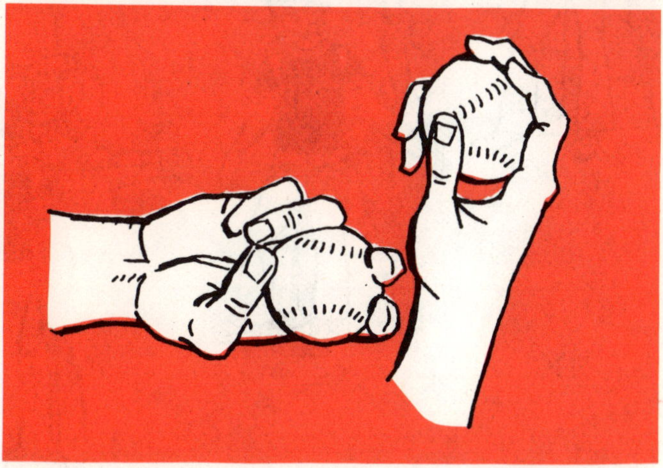

Put your index finger, middle finger and (if it feels good) your ring finger on top of the ball. Your thumb goes underneath. (Of course, this is only true for a ball you can hold in one hand.)

When you let go of the ball to throw it, follow through so the fingers that are on top of the ball end up pointing directly at the target.

**Do you just stand facing the target?**

Definitely not. Stand sideways, with the ball in one hand and the opposite foot in front. (Ball in your right? Then your left foot's in front.)

Gerri Schulman (head of the physical education department of Virgil Junior High School, Los Angeles) works with lots of kids who aren't happy with the way they throw a ball. Roy and Gerri agree that the secret to

throwing well is knowing what it *feels* like to throw well. Then you can do it every time. Gerri says that the trick is to stay as loose as possible.

Imagine that your arm is a very long whip with a moving end. What you are going to do is throw your entire arm at the target.

To get the feeling of a good throw, Gerri urges you to have someone stand behind you, holding your throwing hand. Make sure that your arm is really relaxed. Then have this person bring your arm back, around, over, and then actually *throw your hand*. If you stay loose and do this a couple of times, you'll find that your muscles will get the idea.

*Shawn and Mally hit the spot!*

**Are you supposed to keep your eye on the ball—as everybody says?**

No. That's what you do when you're *catching*. When you throw, look at the place you want to hit. Don't watch the ball!

**Should you try to throw accurately, fast, or far?**

Roy Smalley feels that in most ball games accuracy is first, then speed, then distance.

Practice against a wall or tree. Find or mark a spot on a wall and throw the ball at that spot as hard and as fast as you can. Practice throwing balls through a tire hanging from a tree.

In a game, as you throw, aim for a tiny detail on the first baseman (a letter on his shirt or his belt buckle).

And if you've just caught a ball and have to throw it, transfer it to your throwing hand and *focus* before you throw. Look for a target that's small. (Remember, the catcher holds up a very small target for the pitcher.)

Don't just wait for games to practice. Practice all by yourself.

## CATCHING

**What keeps you from being a good catcher?**

Roy believes that kids are afraid of looking bad. They're afraid of failure. They're afraid of being hurt. He says that professional athletes have the same fears.

The trick is to start easy, and begin with a soft ball (either a solid or hollow one or a tennis ball).

**Is there a secret to catching a ball?**

Catching isn't hard (says Roy). But when the ball comes at them, some kids get tense. The secret is to relax.

**How can you not be afraid as that ball comes whirling at you like a bullet?**

Before you play, look at the ball. Study the seams on

the ball. Look for a mark or a brand name written on it. Then, as it comes hurtling toward you, watch the spinning of those seams. Look for that mark or brand name and watch it until it comes to a stop in your hands.

If you don't think about catching, it's automatic. Train yourself just to *watch the ball all the way into your hands*.

Most catchers start out being afraid of the ball, too. It comes too fast. But if you watch it every inch of the way, it definitely seems to slow it down. Roy says that's even true when you're watching a ball thrown by Nolan Ryan (one of the fastest pitchers in the major leagues).

"The more I watch," Roy says, "the more my watching slows down Ryan's supposedly unhittable ground ball."

Roy has noticed that the best ball players handle the ball before the game, between games, even at home. They finger the ball, they toss it, they hold it. What they're doing is becoming friends with the ball. When you think of an object as a friendly one, you can't be afraid of it.

**How do you catch the ball? Do you just grab it?**

No. Catching is the wrong word. It sounds as if you have to *do* something—like grabbing. A better way to put it would be "cradle" the ball or "receive" the ball.

The idea is to make your hands into two big pillows. You just allow the ball to come into your hands and you cushion it. That's why they say that some catchers have "soft hands." Don't hold out stiff hands and grab for the ball. Just let it come to you, and then "give" with the ball.

**How should you hold your hands?**

Use both hands in a cup-like position. Cup your hands upward.

Decide where the ball is heading and move your body in front of the ball. Don't reach out your hands to the place where you think the ball will land.

Of course, if you find that you can't quite get there, and the ball is going to one side of you—then use one hand.

Roy Smalley started by playing in Little League. He knew he was going to be a ball player when he was five years old. His father played big league ball with the Chicago Cubs and the Philadelphia Phillies.

After a lifetime on the ball field, he's sure that the secret is practice, practice, practice. He says there's no substitute for doing it over and over again.

# 5. Be a Whiz with a Frisbee

"Throwing a Frisbee is 50 percent confidence and 50 percent practice," says Mark Danna, the regional director in New York City for the International Frisbee Disc Association.

The only way to become handy with a Frisbee is to get out there and toss it around. You'll get the hang of it soon enough.

**Do you have to be strong to be a good Frisbee player?** Mark, a former National Frisbee Champion, says you only need a strong wrist. When you throw a Frisbee, it looks like one smooth move, but actually you start by curling your wrist back toward you. Then you hold back. You hold back some more, and finally you *snap* your wrist—and away it flies!

**What's the best way to hold a Frisbee?**

Mark urges you to use any grip that's comfortable—but there's one MUST: Your index finger (your pointer) must extend along the lip (the outer rim) of the Frisbee.

And when you snap your wrist and throw the disc, *it will go wherever you point that index finger*.

**Should you catch the Frisbee with one hand or two?**

Here are the three basic catches:

1. As if you were applauding vertically (up and down), bring one hand up and the other hand down on the Frisbee.

2. As if you were applauding the regular way (sideways), bring both hands together on the outer rim of the Frisbee.

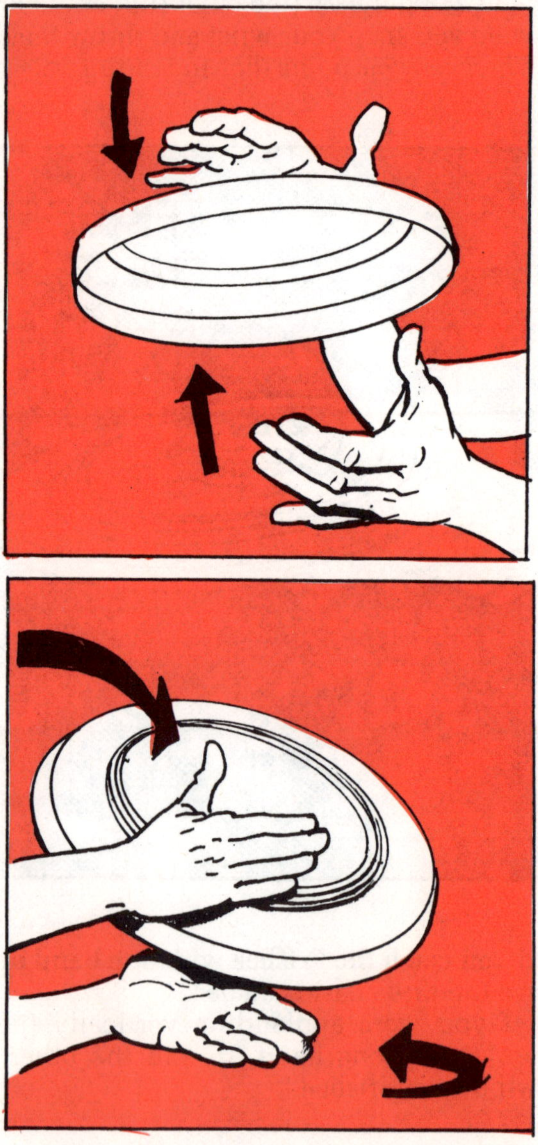

3. To do the standard one-hand catch, shape your fingers into a "C." Then *snap* the thumb and fingers together, closing them on the Frisbee. (Do you know that humans and the apes are the only creatures on earth with thumbs that work in this way?)

**Where's the best place to play?**

On level ground, if possible. Keep your eye on things around you—trees, holes in the ground, rocks, fences. It's hard to get hurt with a Frisbee unless you run into something. (Of course, you *can* get a black-and-blue mark if you catch it wrong, but a Frisbee is safer than, say, a baseball—and it's harder to break windows with one, too!)

Try to play where's there little or no wind. Too much wind, and your Frisbee will fly in a weird way. You might see it going up—up—and then suddenly smash to the ground!

The beach is great, as long as the wind isn't too strong. Just watch where you run. You don't want to wind up in someone's bag of potato chips.

**Are there special "throws"?**

The most common is the backhand, and it's the one to practice first:

1. Stand with your body sideways to the target. This isn't a rule; it's just a good idea.
2. Before you throw, stretch your arm out, Frisbee in hand. Point at the target (that's called "sighting").
3. Tilt down the edge that's farthest from your thumb. The stronger the wind, the sharper you should make the angle. Against a really stiff wind, angle the disc so that it's almost up and down—nearly vertical to the ground.
4. Now bring the Frisbee back across your chest. Curl your wrist toward yourself, and when you're ready to throw, shift your weight from your back foot to your front one. Lead with your elbow, snap your wrist and let 'er sail!

If you'd like to learn other throws, check out Mark Danna's book, *Frisbee Players' Handbook* (Parachuting Publications).

Mark offers a few DON'Ts:

Don't turn your wrist over as you throw.

Don't use your arm instead of snapping your wrist.

Don't throw too hard.

Don't lift your back foot off the ground.

Don't throw your disc against rough surfaces. The

discs scuff, and bits of plastic stick up around the edges. These can sometimes be rubbed off with steel wool. But if your Frisbee tears or cracks, don't bother gluing or taping it. The repair won't last, and a damaged Frisbee won't fly as far or control as well.

**Are there games you can play with a Frisbee?**
Here are two of Mr. Danna's favorite games:

1. *Speed Flow*: Two people, standing about 10 yards apart, make as many catches as they can. Two other people, also 10 yards apart, do the same thing. Each couple shouts "1," "2," "3," as each catch is made. The first couple to make the largest number of catches before a Frisbee is dropped is the winner.
2. *Frisbee Golf*: Pick a tree or a post. Throw the disc toward the target. Pick it up wherever it lands and throw it from there. The player who hits the target first with the fewest number of throws is the winner.

**What's more important, throwing far or throwing accurately?**

Mark says it's a good idea to start with *accuracy*. At first, stand 5 yards from your friend. After a couple of throws, stand a little farther apart, say 10 yards. Little by little, increase your distance.

To throw for *distance*, get a running start, crank your arm way back and then let it rip!

**How can you get your dog to play Frisbee with you?**

Dogs are so nimble, they make super Frisbee players. Naturally, they can catch, but they can't throw! To train your dog as a playmate, do it in stages:

1. Use the disc as a water dish for a couple of days, so your pup'll get used to it as a friendly object.

2. Start to play tug-of-war with it.

3. Play "Go Fetch." Roll the disc and your pup will probably run after it, take it in its mouth and bring it back to you.

4. And finally, start with small tosses. With luck, your dog'll catch the Frisbee in midair, between its teeth.

# 6. Draw and Cartoon What You See—And Then Some!

## CARTOONING

**Do you wish you could draw cartoons, but don't know how to start?**

Howard Post draws cartoons for a living. One of his famous comic strips is "The Dropouts" (United Features), and he has written and drawn many TV shows, including "Tom and Jerry" and "Scooby Doo" by Hanna-Barbera.

He says: start cartooning by studying the cartoons you like. Trace them. Then try to do them from memory.

**How do you make your own funny cartoon people?**

Howard urges you to start with *faces*.

Using a dark pencil or felt-tip pen on plain paper, draw three shapes—a circle, an oval, and a rectangle:

Next, play with *noses*. Here are some samples:

*Eyes* and *eyebrows* come in many shapes, and those shapes change according to the way the cartoon character feels.

—To show *surprise*, stretch the pupil and the eye so they are tall. Raise the inner corner of the eyebows.

—For *happiness*, let the pupils disappear (as they do when *you* smile and your eyes crinkle). Spread the eyebrows apart.

—To draw *anger*, turn the eyebrows upside down. Connect them to strong pupils.

—To show sadness, draw eyebrows that are higher in the center.

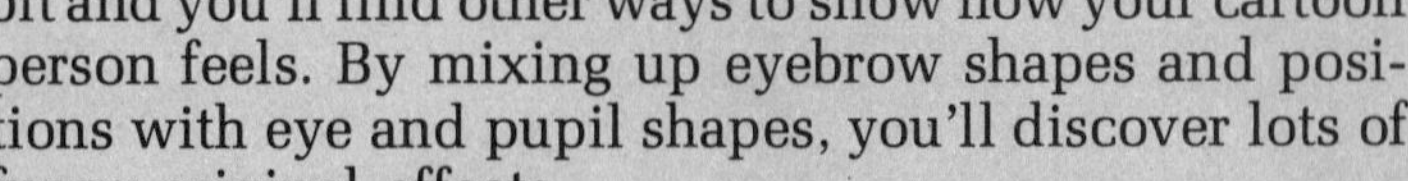

*Surprise* *Happiness* *Anger* *Sadness*

Of course, these are only suggestions. Fiddle around a bit and you'll find other ways to show how your cartoon person feels. By mixing up eyebrow shapes and positions with eye and pupil shapes, you'll discover lots of funny original effects.

And now, on to *mouths*. Let's draw the same feelings that we used with eyes (although people *do* have other feelings besides surprise, happiness, anger and sadness).

Now put the features together.

Play with the distance between the eyes and between the eyes and the nose. Make it close enough to be believable, yet far enough to look a bit weird.

*Happiness* *Anger* *Sadness*

When you can draw a front view of the face that puts a smile on *your* face, try some *side views*. Into the same kinds of shapes, put the same kinds of funny eyes, eyebrows, noses, and mouths.

*Bodies* can begin with a circle, oval, or rectangle too. You might want to add a fourth shape—the *pear shaped* body.

Here are a few funny *feet* samples.

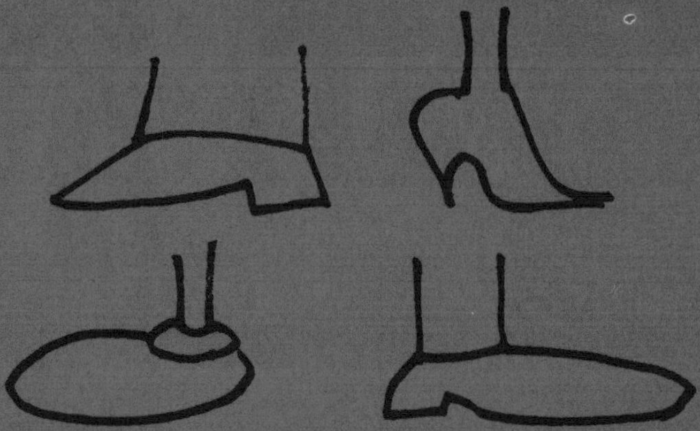

**If you still don't like the cartoons you're drawing, what should you do?**

Howard Post says, "Throw 'em away and do some more!"

## DRAWING

A couple of hints can't turn you into an artist—but if those lines and squiggles you put down on paper don't come together and make up a picture that *says* what you want it to say, these two games are for you.

**How can you draw a picture that will let the person who looks at it know the feelings you had when you drew it?**

Place a piece of paper on the table so that it is taller than it is wide. Divide the sheet into six squares. In square 1, write *loneliness*; in 2, *anger*; in 3, *happiness*; in 4, *sadness*; in 5, *nervousness*; in 6, *joy*.

Now, in each square, make lines or scribbles or marks (not pictures of things, like toys or flowers). The lines should show the *feeling* that you've written at the bottom of each square. You can use lots of lines or just one. If you wish, you can fill the entire box.

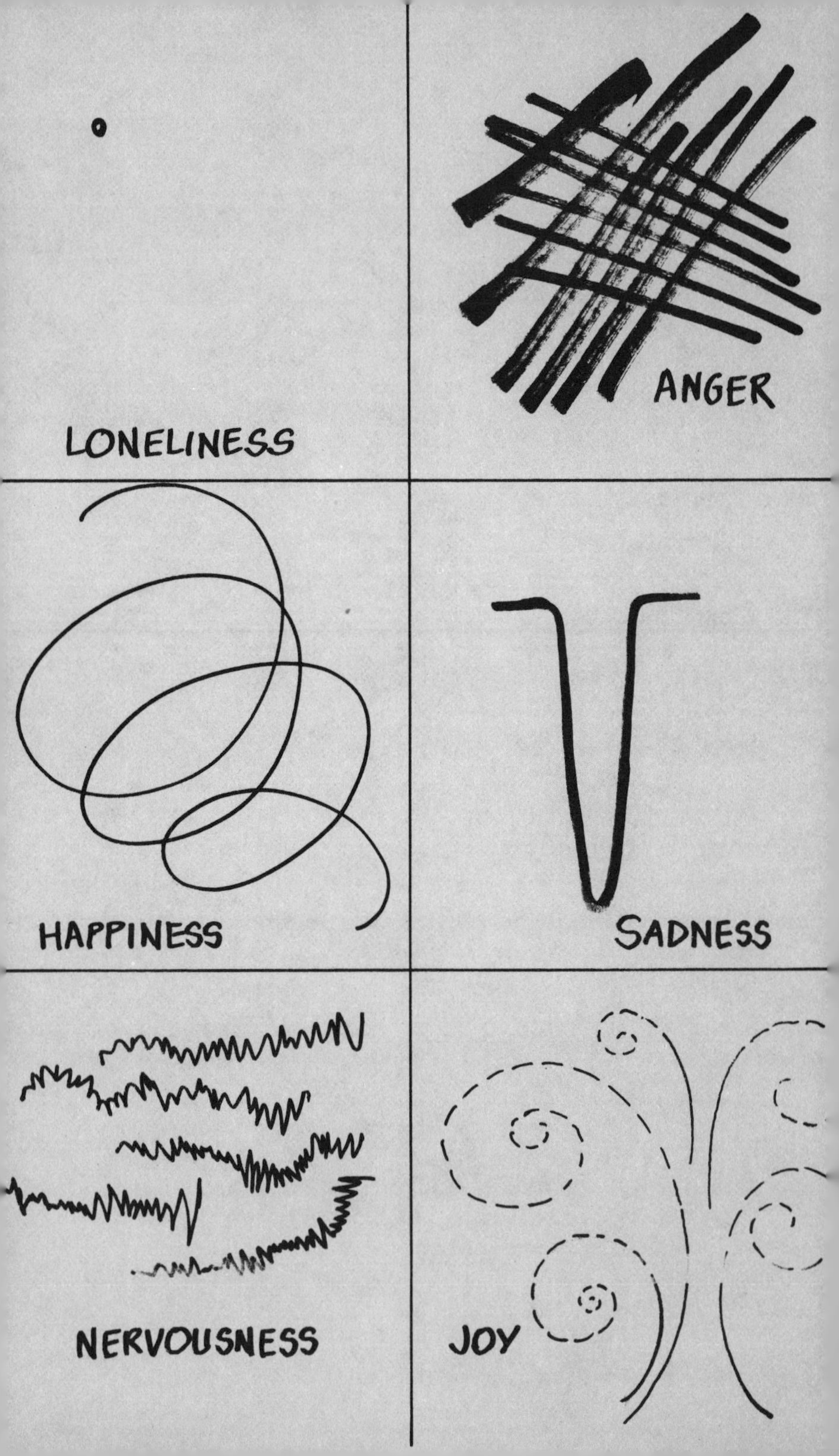
LONELINESS
ANGER
HAPPINESS
SADNESS
NERVOUSNESS
JOY

These are just my drawings—there's no "right" picture of a feeling or emotion. Yours will be different. However, without looking at the word at the bottom of each box, a person looking at your pictures should have some idea of what feeling you're trying to show.

**How can you draw bodies that aren't "flatsies"?** Draw lines that go round and round. Move your pencil quickly. Use your full hand, arm and wrist, not just your fingers. Draw these circular lines to form a skinny pipe, fat pipe and a cone.

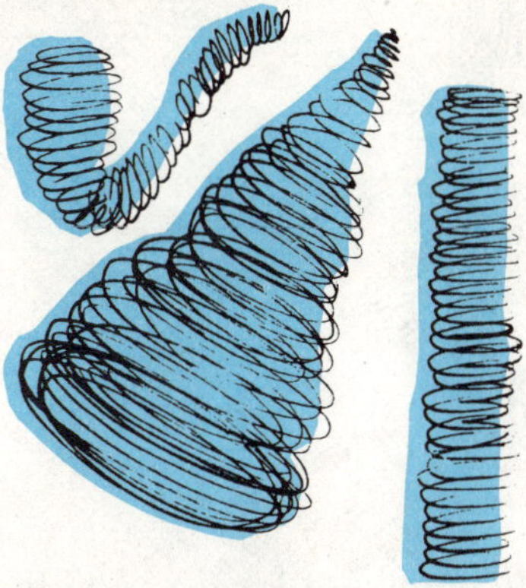

Look at some things around you. Using these fast circular lines, draw a ball or an apple. Draw a pear or a vase. Scribble a lamp with a base and a shade.

Now, using this same motion and circular line, draw one of your friends. Ask your pal to sit still for just a few moments, and scribble away. Your old teddy bear will sit still for you, even if your friend won't!

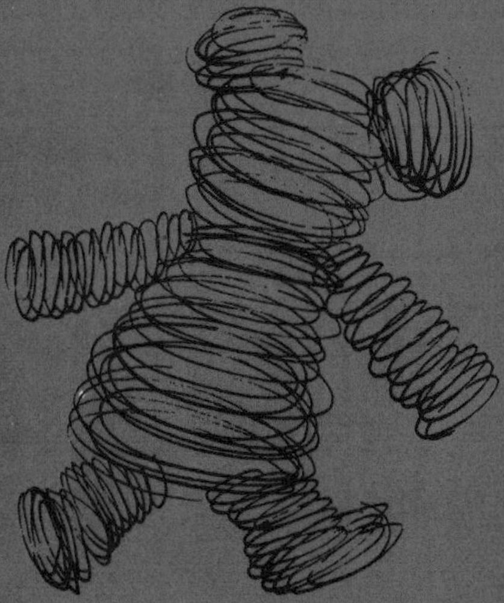

Now, a couple of pages of hints can't turn you into an artist—but these games may help! You can create your picture in private. You can do it and re-do it, and when you *like* it, you can go public and show it to others.

# 7. Getting Animals To Do What You Want Them To Do

It seems as though some people's dogs just can't *wait* to obey their commands, their cats are warm and loving, and when these people walk into a room, even their fish rise to the top of the tank to bubble a welcome.

If you want some secret tips from experts on how to get your dogs, cats, and fish to act as if you too have that "magic touch," read on!

## DOGS

Dick, the Nice Dog Trainer, is what Dick Grossman of Los Angeles calls himself. He and his wife Enid feel that teaching a dog is mere child's play is you keep certain things in mind:

1. Each time you give a command, say the same word *in the same way*. For example, don't say "Down" when you mean "Sit"—or "Quick, get over here" when your dog is used to being told to "Come."
2. Never scold a dog using his or her name (the puppy's name should always be said with friendship and love). In other words, don't say, "Spunky, you're a bad dog!" If Spunky is doing the wrong thing, just say "No!"
3. Don't give a lesson after a meal. That slows down a dog just as it does a person.

**What should you teach your dog first?**

After your dog has learned good manners (which is a polite way of saying that your dog is housebroken), the first thing for a puppy to learn to obey is the command "Sit!"

When Scott Brown, supervisor of training for Dogs for the Deaf in Applegate, Oregon, starts with a new puppy, he puts it on a choke collar and leash, pulls up lightly on the choke collar (this keeps the dog's head up), pushes down on its behind, and says "Sit!" All three—pulling up, pushing down, and command to "Sit!"—happen at the same time.

This is repeated—*firmly*—perhaps four times. As soon as the dog gets fidgety, Mr. Brown stops.

When the dog begins to get an inkling of what "Sit!" means, Mr.Brown *praises* it. He hugs the puppy, raves to it about what a good dog it is, pats it, and so on.

**How do you let your dog know it can stop sitting?**

As the dog is sitting, Mr. Brown releases it by clucking his tongue (the way you cluck to a horse to make it go faster).

Later, when the pup learns to stay, he releases it from *that* command by clucking, too. The dog will learn that it must hold whatever position it's in until it hears these clucks.

**Once your dog can sit, how do you teach it to lie down?**

Mr. Brown says to go back to step 1—get it to *sit* and *praise* it.

Then, hold the leash and pull the dog's head down to the ground. At the same time say, "Lie down!" Repeat this four or five times, praising each time the puppy stays down, even if it's just for a moment. Then release the puppy from the position by clucking.

**How do you get the dog to really stay in one spot?**

Start with the first command, "Sit!" Then say, "Stay!"

and walk away to the end of the leash. If the puppy gets up (chances are, it will), set it right back down again and say, "Stay." Once again, walk to the end of the leash. When your puppy rises again, say, "No!" Set it down and say, "Stay!"

When your dog seems (more or less) to have mastered "Stay," praise it.

Then start walking around the dog, holding the leash up in the air. The puppy's instinct will be to twist its neck in an effort to follow you around. If the dog breaks the *sit*, firmly (but not angrily) say, "No!" and "Stay!"

Use a *hand signal* here as well. Put the palm of your hand up as if you were getting ready to push open a door. Then push forward and downward toward the dog.

Once the dog gets the idea, gently drop the leash on the ground. Walk a few feet away (perhaps 10 feet). Using the hand signal, keep the dog in this position for about 10 seconds. Then cluck to release the pup, and praise it a whole lot.

Mr. Brown and the Grossmans agree that you certainly shouldn't spend more than five minutes at a time working on each command.

**How do you get a dog to shake hands with you?**

First, say, "Sit!" (And then praise—don't ever forget that.)

Next grab the dog's paw and say, "Shake." Praise, wait a few seconds, and then say, "Shake" again. Wait a moment longer (this will give the dog time to make the connection between the word "Shake" and what's happening to his paw). Now lift the paw once more, shake it, and praise a lot. "Good dog! Oh, what a good dog!"

Sooner or later, the dog will master this, and whenever you say, "Shake" that paw will come up all by itself. And when it does, PRAISE that pup!

**If your puppy runs away when you take the leash off, what should you do?**

Don't run after the dog. Dick Grossman suggests that you *run away* from it instead. Then fall down. Your dog's natural curiosity will make it come back to see what's going on. And before you know it, you'll have the puppy licking your face and playing with you.

If you'd like to train your dog to play Frisbee with you, turn to Chapter 5, "Be a Whiz with a Frisbee."

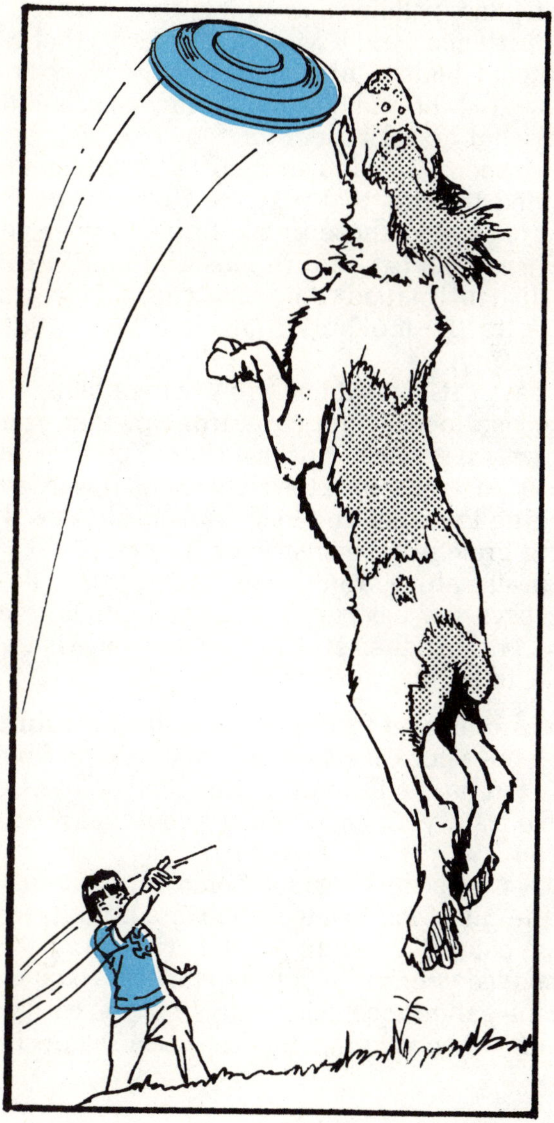

# CATS

**Can you train a cat to obey any commands?**

Moe Di Sesso claims that all it takes is a teaspoon and a lot of patience. And if Moe Di Sesso says that cats can be trained I believe him, because I've worked in TV studios with Moe and his animals for years, and they all do *just* what he asks them to!

You've seen Moe's four-legged TV stars in action, too. He trained the cats that play the banjo in the Friskies commercials, and those in the Buffet Dinner commercial (where each cat, in turn, pushes the next cat away from a dish full of food). And Moe's the man who trained 600 rats for the movies *Willard* and *Ben* — but that's another story!

Moe says cats have their brains in their bellies, so you have to use food as your reward. Not that you don't praise your pet when it does a trick. You do. Cats love affection. After it's done the right thing, reward your cat by rubbing the sides and back of its neck. You'll feel it pressing gratefully against your fingers.

But praise alone won't work with a cat.

Moe says the best time to train a cat is when it's hungry, because then it will do what you wish quickly in order to get the next tidbit.

**How should you feed a cat in order to train it?**

Don't put your cat's food in a dish on the floor. Cats that are fed on the floor think that food comes from the floor. To train your cat, it must know that food comes from *you*.

That's where the teaspoon comes in.

Put the cat's food in a teaspoon and hold it over your lap. The cat will come to *you* for its meal.

If you feed your cat in your lap for say, 10 days (that's where the patience comes in) any time you call, your cat will jump up on your lap. It will—because now it thinks of your lap as the place where food can be found (even if it's not there at that very moment).

When I've worked in TV studios with Mr. DiSesso, I've noticed that his animals watch him very closely. They seem to "read" his body movements. He says that house cats do the same thing, so be sure that your body movements say what you *mean* to say.

For example, if you want the cat to come to you, don't show a fist—that's an aggressive act.

And if the cat often gets food from you as you bend down, don't expect it to stay still when you bend down!

**Can you teach a cat to do real tricks, like "Sit"?**

Once your cat understands that food comes only from you, you can teach your cat to do lots of tricks.

To make it *sit*, put the cat on the floor. Bring the teaspoonful of food toward the cat and then right over its head. In bringing its head back to keep an eye on the food, your cat will automatically sit down. Cats are built that way.

Do it again and again. After a while, whenever you bring your *hand* over its head, your cat will sit.

**How old does a cat have to be before you can train it?**

Most experts say you can't begin to train a cat until it's at least 7 months old. Moe doesn't agree. He trains cats at almost any age. He suggests that you see what you can do with your little kitty as soon as it's away from its mother and on its own.

**What other tricks can cats be taught?**

Make up your own. Want your cat to jump up on a box? Hold the teaspoonful of food over the box. Soon, whenever you hold your *hand* over the box, the cat will jump up.

Want your cat to jump from a chair or countertop down to the floor? Hold your teaspoon on the floor.

Want your cat to jump through a hoop? Hold the teaspoon on the far side of the hoop.

Of course, this will take time. And if things are not going the way they should, try to figure out what might be wrong *from the cat's point of view*.

The cat doesn't want to get hurt. Is the box it's perched on shaky? Is the distance from one box to the other too great? Are you holding the hoop too high?

# FISH

There's not a lot you can train fish to do. I mean, they're just not built to "sit," and you can't expect them to "stay" while treading water!

But at the Aquarium Stock Company in Los Angeles is a man whose name is—and this is the truth—John Fish.

He says there are fish that will come to the surface to be petted (for example, oscars and spring-nose eels). And the Japanese koi-fish (which is a carp) can actually be fed with a baby bottle!

Here are two stunts that John says can be done with almost any old fish.

1. Your fish will ring a bell when they're hungry. Here's what you do:

   Put a little bell on one end of a piece of string. Attach food to the other end of the string and feed your fish by laying the string over the edge of the tank, with the food inside and the bell outside.

After a while, when the fish get hungry they'll nibble on the string. That will pull the string and ring the bell!

2. Your fish will come to the surface to get food whenever you hold up a sign that says "COME AND GET IT."

Each day, hold the sign next to the tank as you drop in the fish food. Take the sign away when the fish stops feeding. In a few days, your fish will come to the top whenever you show the card.

# 8. Taking Photos of the Places, People, and Animals Around You

**Your have a new camera. It looks so complicated—what do you have to know about it?**

Irv Desfor (*Camera Angles* columnist for Associated Press for 31 years) just stared at me when I asked him that question.

"Shari," he said slowly, "if you had a new musical instrument, you'd expect to spend time practicing, wouldn't you? Well, you have to 'rehearse' with a new camera, too."

**Can't you just put in the film and shoot?**

Mr. Desfor assured me that you'd do better to *practice with no film in the camera*. Here's what he suggests:

Handle the camera. Open the back of it. Fiddle with the lens openings. Watch what happens. Put the camera through all its paces. Make every adjustment possible. Set it at every speed. Find out how quickly you can change focus—accurately.

This rehearsal will give you skill with your camera which normally comes only with experience. That will mean you'll be able to grab the best shots in those important moments when you're shooting fast! You'll be able to change the focus instantly in case you want to photograph people or things in the middle of action. You'll *automatically* shift the lens opening if the light changes.

When you're taking a picture, your main attention must be glued to what you're seeing in the viewfinder. The exact instant that things look right in that viewfinder, you CLICK. If you have to think about how the camera works, you'll miss that once-in-a-lifetime picture.

You can also practice *seeing* through the camera without film in it.

—Look for details of closeups which may make better pictures than the whole object (for example, instead of including all the newborn puppies in the basket, perhaps just the mother and the puppy closest to her).

—See if you can find other camera angles than the first (and most obvious) one.

This practice will really pay off when you put film into the camera.

**What kind of film should you use?**

That depends on the camera, the light and the action. But it's best to *start* with black and white film. You'll probably get better results, and it's certainly cheaper as you learn.

**Why do pictures often come out fuzzy and blurry?**

If yours do, you're not alone! Most kids get excited as they shoot. They punch down the release button. This jars the camera and causes the picture to blur.

—Stand with your feet as wide apart as you can comfortably. Then your body almost serves as a tripod for the camera.

—Press the camera firmly against your face or chest and *gently* squeeze the release button. Don't jab it, no matter how exciting the shot.

—Before you squeeze it, *breathe out*. Don't inhale until the shutter is closed.

Never shoot slower than 1/25th of a second, says Mr. Desfor, unless the camera is on a very firm support. Whenever possible shoot at faster speeds. Make your normal speed about 1/100th or 1/125th of a second.

**Do you have to go to so much trouble when taking pictures looks so easy?**

It's no trick to *take* pictures. The fun comes when you *make* pictures.

You *take* them when you are just a button-pusher, snapping away without noticing what's *in back* of the person or object you are shooting, without seeing what's in front, or checking to see if the lighting can be made better.

—Pick a camera angle that cuts out a too-busy background.

—Try not to crowd the image. One way to do this is to get closer.

*Don't pose people stiffly with trees or flag-poles coming out of their heads.*

—Avoid too much stuff or space in front of your subject. (Come in closer to avoid too much sky.)

In other words, you *make* pictures when you fill the frame with a story-telling picture with no unnecessary stuff or blank spaces.

**Do you always have to shoot people as they stand facing bright sunlight?**

No! Mr. Desfor says you can get better pictures in open shade or hazy sun. This will do away with squinty frowns, wrinkled brows and deep shadows around the eyes.

You can use light as it is, or improve it by adding extra light or taking some away.

Today, (he says) if you have a modern camera with a fast lens and fast film, you'll be able to shoot most of your daytime pictures by the light that exists around you. (That's called "available light.") This includes sunlight streaming in a window, a reading lamp in a living room, the overhead fluorescent lamp in the kitchen or office, or the flickering flames of a fireplace.

Available light is *natural* light. It gives your pictures a naturalness that sometimes is lost or changed when artificial light is added. Besides, the people and animals you're photographing will probably be less relaxed if you're fussing with lighting equipment.

If you have an automatic fixed-focus camera (such as a box type), you can't shoot without a flash unless you're in good light.

The nonadjustable cameras generally have a red warning signal that comes on when the flash unit is needed.

Mr. Desfor says that if you are shooting with the flash unit on a box type camera, don't try to grab a picture from more than 12 feet away. (In other words, don't try to shoot the court of a basketball game from your seat in the stands.) He says you *can* get distant shots with the automatic camera, but only with natural light.

And—flash unit or natural light—Irv Desfor urges you not to get closer to your subject than 5 feet with your instamatic type camera.

**How can you tell if you have the right angle for the picture?**

Look through the viewfinder and keep changing your position until the light looks right to you. Maybe you can find an angle where there's side light as well as front light.

Take lots of shots of each picture. Try to tell the picture story from different angles. One of them will turn out to be just right.

**With an automatic camera, how close can you get to the person you're photographing?**

Anything closer than 5 or 6 feet will be out of focus. For sharp pictures at close distances, get a portrait or closeup attachment and add it to the regular lens. Then the distance between you and your subject will have to be measured very carefully, according to the instructions that come with the attachment.

**How can you get sharp pictures when you're shooting people and things in action?**

Action shots are exciting. Nevertheless, resist the urge to jab that release button. No matter how much action is swirling around you, be calm. Gently squeeze that shutter shut.

One good way to get sharper action pictures is to look for the *peak of action*. In many actions, there's a split second where the motion is stopped before it continues. For example, when someone is on a swing, there's a very still moment at the top of the swinging, where the swing has gone as high as it can—and before it starts down.

Focus your camera on that spot where the action stops. Follow the action up to that spot and, in the tiny pause, shoot!

Mr. Desfor suggests that you pick a camera angle at which the action is coming somewhat *toward* you, instead of going across the viewfinder from one side to the other. He says that a shooting speed from 1/125th to 1/200th can stop action in anything coming diagonally toward the camera—like a train, plane, bicycle or someone running.

Pick the spot at which you're going to shoot. When the person or object reaches the spot, push the button.

**How can you get good pictures of little kids or babies?**

Irv Desfor is a real expert at this. My dad is a magician, and since Mr. Desfor was the official photographer for the Society of American Magicians for forty years, all the pictures of me taken during my childhood, *and* all of my daughter's baby pictures, too, were taken by him.

Little children and babies should be photographed when they are in a good mood, like after a nap or a meal. The picture-taking session should feel like play. Here are some hints:

—Give a cookie to the little child.

—Bounce a balloon off the baby's head and off yours.

—Touch honey to the baby's fingertips and let the baby lick the honey off.

—Play hide and seek.

—Build a tower of blocks, and let the child topple them over.

—Use hand puppets.

—Give the little kid a pair of eyeglasses.

—Hide pennies in a book or purse and let the little one find the hidden treasures.

Through all of this, you'll be shooting and getting wonderful expressions and actions, and when the child is tired of playing games, the photo session is over!

**How can you get animals to sit still long enough to take pictures of them?**

The best way (according to Mr. Desfor) is to start with the animal up on a table or bench, so that it can't wander.

What you want to do is *interest* the animal with unusual noises, but not *scare* it with loud ones. You can bark, whistle, crumple cellophane, snap your fingers—do anything you *can* to keep its interest. And when the animal reacts, shoot!

Food, or the *smell* of food can be used to keep a pet on your "stage set."

In winter, cats prefer a warm spot near a radiator or in the sun on the rug or window sill.

The best help of all in shooting animals is to get yourself an assistant. This person can keep the pet's attention, serving as a noise maker (*as you shoot away*), and will also be able to fetch the animal if it jumps off the perch. Meanwhile, you can concentrate on looking for that perfect moment.

**What's the best kind of camera to carry on vacation?**

For travel, Mr. Desfor believes in the boy scout motto: "Always be prepared." Keep your camera loaded at all times, focused at 15 feet.

"A camera that isn't loaded," he says, "might just as well be home on the shelf." On vacations, picture-taking chances appear suddenly. That great picture is before your eyes only an instant and then it vanishes.

Cameras in luggage are no help when that "perfect moment" arises.

Never tuck the camera away in the glove compartment or trunk of the car. They can become hot boxes and ruin film.

Never take a new or borrowed camera on your vacation trip without testing it first and getting to know how it works. Use at least one roll (more if possible) indoors and out, and study the results at home before you leave.

**Can I shoot pictures from the TV screen?**

Irv Desfor does it all the time. Here's the secret:

—Your camera should be on a tripod or firm support.

—Focus only on the screen.

—Use the fastest black and white or color film. For an instamatic camera, use ASA 400 film (black and white or color). It's very fast.

—Set the shutter speed at only 1/30th or 1/25th of a second, no faster. Adjust the lens opening according to the meter.

—*Do not use a flash.* (It wipes out the entire picture on the screen.)

—Turn off all the room lights, because they reflect off the TV screen.

Georgia tells a good story at her slumber party.

# 9. Cracking Jokes and Telling Stories

**What's the best way to begin a funny story?**

Never start by saying, "Hey, this is a funny story." When kids are told that a joke is going to make them laugh, they often sit back and (without saying so) almost *dare* you to be funny! Better to introduce the joke *as* you tell it, and surprise 'em with the funny part (the punch line) at the end.

That's what Marty Ragaway says and he should know! Marty has written for lots of great TV comics (Dick Van Dyke, Red Skelton and Alan King, among 'em). He's now the publisher of *Funny Funny World*, a newsletter about the funny things happening around the world.

**How do you get people to want to listen to you as you tell funny stories?**

"If you're telling a joke to a group, tell a little bit to each person. Look right *at* the person you are talking to," says Michael Binder, a young comic from The Comedy Store in Los Angeles.

**Should you laugh as you tell your own jokes?**

Well, don't be straight-faced or grim about it (unless you're telling a grim story). Smile—get into the spirit of the thing. If you're having fun telling it, chances are the listener will have fun hearing it. But don't laugh as you tell the punch line, because you really want your friends to understand it!

**If you're not sure people will listen all the way through the story, should you talk fast?**

Rushing through comedy is not a good idea. After all, *you* know what's coming because you've heard it before —but to the listener, it's probably the first time, so speak clearly and take your time.

**Can you tell a favorite funny story more than once?**

You can, but not to the same audience! Even terrific jokes only make you laugh hard the *first* time you hear them. If you love a joke, tell it to everyone you meet— once.

**Should you add details to a joke to make it interesting and really juicy?**

No, no, no. Make each joke as short as possible. If *you* wander, your audience will lose track of what you're saying and where you're going. (David Couwlier, another funny young man from The Comedy Store, feels very strongly about this.)

**Should you memorize a joke before you tell it?**

"Not really," says David.

A funny story has a "set up" and "punch line." The set up is all the stuff the listener has to know in order to get the *point* of the story, which comes at the end—with, you hope, a real sock to it—which is why it's called a *punch line*.

You should know (but not memorize) all the basic points of the set up. But include only what is needed to make the punch line work. Too much information will confuse the punch line.

However, anything that needs to be known for that punch line should be said at least twice. Marty Ragaway stressed that. He told me this joke that you TV commercial watchers may like:

> *Kay died. And at Kay's funeral someone sighed "Poor Kay" and the casket lid opened and a little voice muttered "Butter!"*

KIDS-ONLY
POOR KAY BUTTER

(Say it out loud and you'll get it. It's a pun on the Parkay Margarine commercials.)

Now her name (Kay) has to be said twice before the punch line ("Poor Kay" — "Butter").

That punny joke is what comics call a groaner. Marty thinks that people hearing puns groan because they wish *they* had said it!

Now, David urges you not to memorize your funny material, because a good joke should sound as if you are making it up right then and there, *as* you are telling it.

But all three experts agree that there's one exception to that rule: you *must* remember your old friend, *the punch line*. You don't want to get all the way through the story and then forget how it ends. So you can memorize just that punch line!

**Do all jokes have to end in punch lines?**

Pretty much. Funny tales generally end with a snapper, a twist, something you don't expect, which makes you laugh as much in surprise as at the story itself.

**What's a good way to remember all the good jokes you've heard when you want to tell them?**

Cut out a tiny card. On it put just two or three words for each joke to help remind you. Carry this card in your wallet. You can bring to mind a dozen or so jokes just by peeking at the card.

**How can you get up enough nerve to tell a joke?**

Don't start with strangers. After you tell the story to your mirror and the tape machine, try it out on your sister, brother, mom, dad, or best friend.

**What kind of jokes should you tell? Which do kids like best?**

Jokes in which one person is just plain dumb — the dumber the better! This kind of comedy has been around forever. Hundreds and hundreds of years ago, the "dummy" was usually the "clod" or country bumpkin. Nowadays, the butt of the joke sometimes turns out to be the city slicker who (according to this kind of humor) really can't do basic things for himself. For example:

> *A man from the city bought a farm. The old farmer tried to be really helpful and said, "You can call on me any time." The city guy moved to the farm. About a month later the farmer got a phone call from the city slicker, who said, "Will you sell me some more chickens?" The farmer asked, "What happened to the ones you had?" The city fellow said, "I don't know–I either planted them too close together or too deep."*

Lots of these "don't-know-nothin'" stories can be made even funnier by telling them as if they really happened to people you know. For example, in telling the story about planting chickens, you might say, "I've been told that years ago, before I was born, my grandfather sold his farm —." If you can trick people into thinking that the story is one that really happened, the silly twist at the end will be even more of a surprise.

**Should you act out the characters in the joke?**

Why not? You can change the expression on your face or the tone of your voice according to the character. Papa Bear can have a loud deep voice, Goldilocks might have one that is high and squeaky, or vice versa!

Sometimes these funny characters you act out will be so good they will get big laughs in themselves. That's okay, but do be careful. If you get laughs *right before* your punch line, it will probably cut down on the amount of laughter you get at the end of your story.

After you've told the story a few times, you might choose to be not quite so funny *on the way* to the punch line, and save the big laugh for the end.

**Why do you sometimes only get a chuckle when you thought you told a really funny joke?**

That doesn't mean that the joke wasn't good or well told. There are different kinds of laughter, and sometimes a giggle or groan can mean that you have satisfied your audience—even though you may not have satisfied yourself!

Every comic I know agrees on one thing: To make your audience laugh, you should relax, take your time and enjoy what you're doing. Telling jokes should be as much fun for you as it is for the lucky person listening to you.

## STORYTELLING

**Is storytelling different from joke telling?**

When you think about it, it is! If I sound surprised when I say that, it's because *I* never thought about it.

As a performer, I tell stories whenever that's a part of my show. But they're not *my* stories. They're Hans Christian Andersen's stories, or Mark Twain's stories, or other stories written by somebody else. I think *anybody* with a nice speaking voice and a little nerve can do that.

When you get finished telling somebody else's story, you haven't shared any of yourself.

There's another kind of storytelling that I like even better. A friend of mine, an actor named Troy Evans, showed me this other way.

Troy comes from Montana. When he tells my daughter and me tales of the Montana winter snows and of copper mines and mountain paths, we can see other places, people— even other times.

Now, Troy feels that there are probably only two good reasons to tell a joke—to make people laugh or to make a point.

But there are lots of different reasons to tell a story. You can:

—Bring back a moment or an event that you remember.

—Give information.

—Share a bit of yourself, and tell the listener how you feel about things.

A joke is different from a story in other ways too.

—A joke has a set up and a punch line.

—A story has a beginning, a thread, and some kind of ending, not necessarily *punchy*.

—A joke should be as short as possible, while a story can have lots and lots of *details*.

Troy loves details in his stories. But he urges you to be specific, not general. Instead of describing a man as "a very big man," paint a clearer picture. (".... He was six feet, five inches tall. He weighed three hundred and thirty pounds!")

And Troy urges you *not to exaggerate*! Don't say, "The event was the greatest," or, "This character is the richest." That just gets boring. It also challenges the listeners to compete with you. ("That was the greatest game," you say—and your listener thinks, "Hey. I once saw a great game, too.")

Troy Evans is careful with the details in his stories. They have to help the point of the story and not the *background* of the story. Don't wander too far off the point.

For example, if you're telling the story of Joseph and his striped coat (in which Joseph's father liked him the best of all the sons, and gave him the beautiful striped coat, and his jealous brothers tried to get rid of him—remember?), don't drag out the description of *how far* they took Joseph to get rid of him, or of what the brothers *looked* like, or the roughness of the road over which they traveled, or what they ate, or what the weather was like!

The thread has to go through from the beginning of

the story to the end. It can curve, but there can't be big knots of details along the way.

**What's the best time to tell a story?**

A joke is lively. You can often stop people in their tracks with "Did you hear the one about— ?"

A story is different. Troy says you have to pick the right time to tell a story. You can't just slip it in the way you can a joke. You can't corner folks when they're trying to make a meal or do other things. A good time to tell a story is:

—over dinner

—at parties (particularly slumber parties)

—at the beach

—on long car, bus, train, or plane trips

—on walks

If you have a really good story that you feel like telling, perhaps you can persuade the folks around you to turn off the TV set.

**Where can you find tales to tell?**

Grandparents often have fantastic yarns about the old ways, the old times, the old country. Some of these really-truly stories are so unbelievable to us today that they sound made up!

Often, old folks have told their children and grandchildren the same favorite tales for years. (Troy's grandfather lived on the other side of the mountains. He only visited them on holidays. Each Christmas he would come through the mountain pass all excited because he had just met Santa Claus at the top of the hill, and Santa Claus had filled the back of his car with gifts for the children. You may not believe that story, but Troy and his sisters and brothers still loved to hear it!)

Troy says the best way to become a good storyteller, and have lots of good yarns to spin is:

—Really listen to the stories others tell and to the things people say.

—Remember your dreams.

—Look at what's happening around you.

Driving with Troy Evans the other day, we passed my postman. I told Troy that this postman is a cranky man, an unfriendly person. He really doesn't like his work, and in the rainy season he even leaves our mail and magazines out where they get wet.

However, as we passed the postman, he was gently bending over to pet a couple of dogs. They had come out to greet the postman, who obviously was their friend.

It was very interesting to see the other side of this cranky, crotchety man.

Now, that's a story with no ending—it was just interesting. The next day, I heard Troy telling it to my daughter at the lunch table, and she was truly fascinated to know that our postman had another side to him.

That's a nice kind of story.

**What do you do if you want to tell people about the TV shows and movies you've seen, but nobody wants to listen?**

You can't really tell a whole movie or TV show well. And nobody's got enough time to listen to the whole thing! If you really love something that you've seen, stop for a minute. Figure out what's the most important part of it. What scene did you love? What funny thing did the character say? Tell only those things that give the special flavor of the show, and you'll find that people will listen with interest.

# 10. Make Your Own Kids-Only Club T-Shirt

If you'd like to have the Kids-Only Club design running across your T-shirt, too, here's how you can do it:

Place wax paper on top of this Kids-Only Club design

(the words are printed backwards so when you transfer this design to your shirt, they will be right). Trace it in pencil. With dark crayons, go over the outline and the details on the wax paper. Brush away extra flecks of crayon.

Slip a shirt cardboard or small bread board inside a T-shirt to stretch the fabric a bit. Place your design *crayon side down* on the T-shirt.

Ask an adult to set the iron temperature selector for the kind of material you are using. Press the iron to the wax paper briefly (don't move it back and forth). The heat will melt the crayon and the outline will be transferred to the shirt. Take away the paper and look at what you've done.

The outline won't be sharp. Take your crayons and color in the outline and design directly on the T-shirt, pressing hard with your crayons.

Now you have to "fix" the crayoning. With the board still in the shirt, place a fresh piece of wax paper under the shirt fabric where you have crayoned. The paper should be between the board and the inside of the shirt. Place another piece of wax paper *over* your design. Once again iron—very slowly this time—over the top sheet of the paper. The heat will melt the heavy crayoning you have put on the T-shirt, and it will really sink in.

Once your crayon colors have been ironed in, your Kids-Only Club T-shirt can be hand washed again and again in cold or lukewarm water and the colors will neither run nor fade. But don't put it in with other laundry.

# Index

KIDS-ONLY CLUB
KIDS-ONLY CLUB
KIDS-ONLY CLUB
KIDS ONLY CLUB
Bye see you soon